Transforming Lives

Advent Meditations
Four Weeks of Spiritual Meditation
and Reflection

Isaac N. Hudson, II

and

Mary A. Hudson

First Edition

NEWMAN SPRINGS PUBLISHING
320 Broad Street
Red Bank, NJ 07701

First originally published by Newman Springs Publishing 2020

ISBN 978-1-64531-992-4 (Paperback)
ISBN 978-1-64531-993-1 (Digital)

Printed in the United States of America

In Matthew's gospel, Jesus uses the metaphor of "light" to describe who we are as followers of Jesus the Christ...a light as a city on a hill that cannot be hidden (Matthew 5:14).

We share this meditation for the reader to be inspired to develop a more intimate relation with our creator through Jesus Christ, our Lord and Savior. This meditation is presented to complement your daily readings, that your light will shine brightly both personally and communally. Twenty-eight days are included for Advent meditations. We celebrate daily the revelation of Christ's presence, power, and authority through the Holy Spirit. We are thankful and excited to pause to celebrate Christ's coming into the world as the prophets foretold. The prophets declared the love and promise of God.

Today, believers declare, "What a mighty God we serve." Today, believers declare that angels bow before him, heaven and earth adore him, what mighty God we serve!

We are awakened daily to a chaotic world. We are awakened daily to the reality of a society which appears to have shifted the tradition norms and means to unacceptable politics, practices, and norms. Nonetheless, the believer awakens to the reality that Jesus Christ is the same yesterday, today, and forever more.

In this season, we continue to anticipate his coming to do what he has always done and that is to bring light and life into a dark world. In the Advent, his presence will transform lives. He will set at liberty the captive, mend the broken hearted, and give sight to the blind in the world. He will proclaim the acceptable year of the Lord, and he will heal those wounded by social, political, and economic ungodly forces (Luke 4:18–22).

We encourage you to read with the hope of transformation. Read, pray, praise, and expect the great God to be present through the manifestation of the Holy Spirit. Expect the great God to do great things in your life. Allow this manifestation to so fill you and others that the light of his presence will dispel the world's darkness, moment by moment, day by day, and one by one.

Be transformed!

Acknowledgments

This meditation is written to inspire others to develop a more intimate relationship with Jesus the Christ, Son of God. We have loved, prayed, studied, and labored in the field for forty-four years. I thank God for our many opportunities to share in life, marriage, and ministry. Our experiences over the years have been influenced by our children Eric, Isaac III, Ikeisha, and Ivan, our grandchildren, other family members, friends, and yes, our faith members.

Thanks to each of you that will read and buy the meditation booklet. Many blessings!

Isaac and Mary A. Hudson

Week I

Light the Candle of: Hope

Sunday: Thought for Today: The Lord is the light of my life.

Scripture: Romans 13:11–14

Meditation: In the story of creation, the Bible teaches us that God dispelled the darkness by creating the sun to rule by day and the moon and stars to rule by night. God's desire was that humankind would not live in darkness. During this Advent Season, let us be reminded that God is love and light, in him there is no darkness. Because humans are the crowning work of God's creation, we should live in the light as people of light. We dare not live in fear, ignorance, doubt, or hopelessness. "The Anointed Christ of God" has come as the light of our salvation; therefore we live in faith, knowledge, confidence, righteousness, and hope eternal! The darkness of sin will not have dominion over my life. Let us pray!

Prayer: Precious Lord, you are holy indeed! Grant me the wisdom to walk in the light of your Word that I may please you and honor you with my being. In the name of Jesus I pray. Amen

Daily Reflections

What does the scripture mean to me?

____

____

____

____

____

How will I apply this meditation and bring light to my day?

____

____

____

____

____

What will I be able to share with others to help them to know Christ?

____

____

____

____

____

Monday: Thought for Today: God is faithful and just.

Scripture: I Corinthians 1:3–9

Meditation: This Monday help others to know that the God we serve is faithful and just. The apostle Paul reminds us that "we have been called into fellowship with the Lord Jesus Christ." How exciting it is to know that because of his love relationship, our God will always be faithful and just. He will forgive our sins and cleanse us from unrighteousness when we repent and sincerely surrender to his will and way. He will strengthen us in our weakness and temptation, and will reveal himself to us. God's abiding presence will comfort us because God is faithful. Let us pray!

Prayer: Dear Jesus, consecrate me that I may stand blameless before you. Enrich my life that I might know your truths and daily strive to glorify you in my living. In the name of Jesus I pray. Amen

Daily Reflections

What does the scripture mean to me?

____

____

____

____

____

How will I apply this meditation and bring light to my day?

____

____

____

____

____

What will I be able to share with others to help them to know Christ?

Tuesday: Thought for Today: Watch for his coming.

Scripture: Mark 13:33–37

Meditation: Today is the day we reflect on spiritual alertness. From time to time we are challenged by adversarial dynamics in life that will lure us to sleep or cause us to doubt the presence and power of God. *Not today*! Today, we affirm that we will always be on guard for our very life depends on it. God has given us everything we need to overthrow the enemy in our lives. God has entrusted his ministry and works to his people and equips us for good works. Be alert, be on guard, keep watch, and be steadfast over the things of God. Let us pray!

Prayer: Dear Jesus, master of my house. Let me hear your voice so sweet. Help me to be watchful, to be on my guard! Help me to stay awake! Here I am, Lord. Speak to my heart in the holy season. Let me watch and wait for you to come. Come, O Holy Christ, and dwell among us. I wait patiently to hear from you. Speak and my soul will hear. In the name of Jesus I pray. Amen

Daily Reflections

What does the scripture mean to me?

____

____

____

____

____

How will I apply this meditation and bring light to my day?

____

____

____

____

____

What will I be able to share with others to help them to know Christ?

____

____

____

____

____

Wednesday: Thought for Today: Jesus is the light of the world.

Scripture: John 1:1–5

Meditation: Alleluia! This day, know that we have the light of the world. This light cannot be extinguished, nor can it be hidden. This light is the Word of God, and was with God in the beginning before anything was made. Alleluia! This light which was and is the Word of God is named Jesus, the "Anointed Christ of God." This Jesus is life and this life is the light of humankind. He is our light in a world of darkness, cruelty, hate, anger, and death. We are summoned to live in the light now and forever. Shine light, shine on me! Let us pray!

Prayer: O Lord of light and love, thank you for the Word made flesh. Let your Word live in me so I can live for you that men might see my good works but glorify you in heaven. Amen.

Daily Reflections

What does the scripture mean to me?

____

____

____

____

____

How will I apply this meditation and bring light to my day?

____

____

____

____

____

What will I be able to share with others to help them to know Christ?

____

Thursday: Thought for Today: The illuminating light of Jesus shines in the darkest places of the world.

Scripture: John 1:6–9

Meditation: Awake, sleeping people! Awake, fearful people! Awake, frustrated and doubting people! Awake from hating on self and others. The long dark night is over, if you will believe and accept the reality of the "Love and Light of God" whose name is Jesus. John the Baptist came as a witness and a consecrated forbearer of the good news, that the light of the world was setting the stage for an eternal presence. Today, we live with the presence and power of God through God's saving, redeeming, and illuminating light, Jesus the Christ. Let us pray!

Prayer: God of grace and God of glory. Create in me a clean heart Oh God, and renew a right spirit within me. Let me live that you will trust me to bear the truth of your Word. In the precious name of Jesus I pray. Amen

Daily Reflections

What does the scripture mean to me?

____
____
____
____
____

How will I apply this meditation and bring light to my day?

____
____
____
____
____

What will I be able to share with others to help them to know Christ?

____

____

____

____

____

Friday: Thought for Today: O Christ of God, descend upon my heart.

Scripture: Jeremiah 33:14–16

Meditation: The prophecy of Jeremiah to Judah and Jerusalem was that God would fulfill his promise. The promise that Judah would be saved and Jeremiah would live in safety would be fulfilled through the presence and power of "the Lord, our Righteousness." God promised that at his coming, he would do what is just and right. We are comforted in knowing that God will do for us what is just and right. Be encouraged today! Go forth now and in the future, believing that all things are possible because of him who loved you first. His name is Emmanuel! Let us pray.

Prayer: O gracious Father God, thank you for the unmerited favor you bestowed upon me. You loved me so much that you allowed me to become one of your children. Thank you, Lord, that I have a rich heritage and a place in your eternal kingdom. In the holy name of Jesus, I pray. Amen.

Daily Reflections

What does the scripture mean to me?

____

____

____

____

____

How will I apply this meditation and bring light to my day?

____

____

____

____

____

What will I be able to share with others to help them to know Christ?

____

____

____

____

____

Saturday: Thought for Today: The Lord is the everlasting light.

Scripture: Isaiah 60:19–22

Meditation: Isaiah has declared, "For the Lord will be your lasting light, and your God will be your glory." The Psalmist declared, "The Lord is the strength of my life, of whom shall I fear?" Today, let us walk by faith with courage and purpose because the light of God is everlasting. This light is our salvation and strength for the living of the days and for the glory which belongs to God. Hallelujah, thine be the glory. Hallelujah, amen! Let us pray!

Prayer: God of love and light, thank you for your grace. Thank you for lighting this world with your Son. Thank you for his shining example for my life. May the Lord of lights use the little light I have and allow it to fan into flames of hope that the world may be brighter because of you. I love you, Lord. Amen.

Daily Reflections

What does the scripture mean to me?

____
____
____
____
____

How will I apply this meditation and bring light to my day?

____
____
____
____
____

What will I be able to share with others to help them to know Christ?

____
____
____
____
____

Week II

Light the Candle of: Love

Sunday: Thought for Today: The "Day of the Lord" is upon us.

Scripture: Isaiah 11:1–10

Meditation: Isaiah's text completes the prophecy spoken in chapter 10 through chapter 12:6, that God would destroy Assyria. The one who is to come will not judge with the physical eyes or ears; but he will see and hear with righteousness and justice for the needy, poor, excluded, downtrodden, persecuted, and wounded in spirit. Righteousness will be his belt and faithfulness the sash around his waist. Let us proclaim today from mountain tops and valleys that our God is faithful, and just, and will always keep his promise. Alleluia! Proclaim for the suffering people of Haiti, the people of West Africa whose lives are in jeopardy each day, the people of the Virgin Islands who constantly live with the threat of natural disasters. Proclaim that God is faithful and more than able to even bring their enemies to their aide and rescue. Isaiah reminds us that the "earth will be full of knowledge of the Lord God Almighty." Thank God for his awesome power. He is still making a way out of no way. Let us pray!

Prayer: God of grace and God of glory, on your people pour your power! As we anticipate the birth of the Prince of Peace, prepare us, O prepare us for this glorious day when you rain down justice and peace on your crowning work of creation! In the holy name of Jesus, I pray. Amen! Amen! Amen!

Daily Reflections

What does the scripture mean to me?

____
____
____
____
____

How will I apply this meditation and bring light to my day?

____
____
____
____
____

What will I be able to share with others to help them to know Christ?

____
____
____
____
____

Monday Thought for Today: God is present among us.

Scripture: Zephaniah 3:14–17

Meditation: Today, my brothers and sisters, shout, sing, rejoice, and be glad in your heart. The Lord forgives sin, takes away punishment, and destroys your enemies. The Lord's coming provides salvation and safety because he loves us. Through the presence and power of Emmanuel (God with us) we do not succumb to the enemies of fear, depression, apathy, poverty, hatred, war, greed, and starvation. God is mighty to save. Rejoice through your suffering for he has come and he is coming. Great God, Mighty Savior, Anointed Christ, comforting Holy Spirit, thank you! Let us pray!

Prayer: O, omnipresent God. I am humbled in your presence. Help me in my moments of despair, to always remember that you are ever present. Even when it seems that I can't feel you near, remind me in your own magnificent way, that you are calming me with your love. I love you, Lord! Amen.

Daily Reflections

What does the scripture mean to me?

____

____

____

____

____

How will I apply this meditation and bring light to my day?

____

____

____

____

____

What will I be able to share with others to help them to know Christ?

____

____

____

____

____

Tuesday Thought for Today: God is still working miracles.

Scripture: Matthew 1:18–25

Meditation: Today, believe that God is still working miracles. Sometimes when we attempt to explain the various experiences in our lives, we are often left void of explanation or understanding. Let us share this reality with others, that God transcends time and circumstances and works his supernatural powers and will in our lives. How comforting it is to know that God will bring extraordinary results out of ordinary situations. Trust God today and always. Watch God work a miracle in your situation to his glory and honor. Let us pray!

Prayer: Precious Father, thank you the gift of your dear Son, Jesus the Christ. Thank you for the baby Jesus, gift-wrapped from you to teach us how to live, to show us the light of your love. In his name, I pray. Amen

Daily Reflections

What does the scripture mean to me?

____

____

____

____

____

How will I apply this meditation and bring light to my day?

____

____

____

____

____

What will I be able to share with others to help them to know Christ?

____

____

____

____

____

Wednesday Thought for Today: God is preparing us for his will and his glory.

Scripture: Matthew 2:8–20

Meditation: There are times in life when it seems that our lives are in a "holding pattern." We can't seem to move forward or backward. The time in our lives when we experience this holding pattern is often the time that God is preparing us for his will and his glory. Today, let us be patient and wait on the move of God. When we wait, hold our position, moving only at God's command, only then will we avoid the traps of the enemy. Share with someone today that God has a "preferred future" for their lives. Glory to his name. Let us pray!

Prayer: All wise and all-knowing Father God, what an awesome blessing that you loved the world so much that you sent Jesus to be a light for all the people of the world. So much so that I am a recipient of your grace! Even me, Lord! Even me! Thank you, Father! I love you, Lord! Amen!

Daily Reflections

What does the scripture mean to me?

____

____

____

____

____

How will I apply this meditation and bring light to my day?

____

____

____

____

____

What will I be able to share with others to help them to know Christ?

____

____

____

____

____

Thursday Thought for Today: The light of the Son shines as an overshadowing force in a dark, dark world.

Scripture: Matthew 4:14–16

Meditation: The light is coming, the light is here, the light will return. Rejoice today that the light is come, is here, his name is Jesus—the Anointed Christ of God. We no longer have to live in sin without hope of a deliverer. Rejoice! God's Word is true, and perfect, and right. Jesus Christ is coming into the world for you and for me. Every demonic spirit will surrender and flee. Every hopeless situation will dissipate. Testify to someone today.

Prayer: My Lord and my God, truly I have sinned against you and beg your pardon for my iniquity. Cleanse me, wash me, deliver me, and restore me to a right relationship with you. Come with your strong arms and comfort me with your grace. In the name of Jesus, I pray. Amen.

Daily Reflections

What does the scripture mean to me?

____

____

____

____

____

How will I apply this meditation and bring light to my day?

____

____

____

____

____

What will I be able to share with others to help them to know Christ?

____

____

____

____

____

Friday: Thought for Today: Today, I am reminded again that Jesus is the light of the world.

Scripture: John 9:1–7

Meditation: Today, I want to see more, feel more, share more, and love more of the excellence of God's perfect Word. Didn't you know, God's Word for us today and forever is Jesus the Christ? I want to see more of the beauty of creation and the movement of God's people. I want to feel more love for others, especially the suffering and less fortunate. I want to share more because God loves me, healed my broken spirit, and cleansed me from all unrighteousness. I want more because God has given me so much more. Be encouraged, the "Christ of God" is working miracles. Let us pray!

Prayer: Precious Lord of miracles, I love your perfect Word. Help me in every situation to see the beauty of your Word to work your perfect will in every situation. In the loving name of Jesus I pray. Amen

Daily Reflections

What does the scripture mean to me?

____

____

____

____

____

How will I apply this meditation and bring light to my day?

____

____

____

____

____

What will I be able to share with others to help them to know Christ?

____

____

____

____

____

Saturday: Thought for Today: God's light gives clear direction.

Scripture: Luke 3:1–6

Meditation: Thank you, thank you, for this new morning with your new mercy. Thank you for making the crooked places straight and rough places plain. Today, rejoice with me that we have forgiveness of sins when we repent. Share the good news with someone, anyone that the "Anointed Christ of God" has come into the darkness of sin, fear, and death. His light has dispelled the darkness. His light is for ever and ever, hallelujah!

Prayer: God of clear direction, thank you for illuminating my path. Thank you for showing me the right way, leading me down the straight and narrow path. I bless you for directing my path, and leading, and guiding me with the light of your Word. In the name of Jesus I pray. Amen

Daily Reflections

What does the scripture mean to me?

____

____

____

____

____

How will I apply this meditation and bring light to my day?

____

____

____

____

____

What will I be able to share with others to help them to know Christ?

____
____
____
____
____

Week III

Light the Candle of: Joy

Sunday: Thought for Today: The Light of God in us overshadows the darkness in the world.

Scripture: Isaiah 60:1–3

Meditation: Today, in this Advent Season of our Christian witness, arise and shine, for the light of the incarnate God is upon us. The prophecy is being fulfilled in the lives of God's people again. He has come to defeat the enemies of hate, greed, oppression, depression, loneliness, war, and death. Let us be comforted today in knowing that we are not alone in life's struggles. God is here, Christ is here, the Holy Spirit is here. Seek the light of his countenance that his glory may rest upon you. Be strong, my brother and sister, and be of good courage. The enemies are defeated by the light of God's presence. Let us pray!

Prayer: O giver of life and light, thou glorious light of night and day, thank you for making your way available to all people. I know that it is your will that your light outshines the darkness in this world. Help me to let my little light shine for you. In the name of Jesus I pray. Amen

Daily Reflections

What does the scripture mean to me?

____
____
____
____
____

How will I apply this meditation and bring light to my day?

____
____
____
____
____

What will I be able to share with others to help them to know Christ?

____
____
____
____
____

Monday: Thought for Today: God allows his Word to become convincing through my witness.

Scripture: 2 Corinthians 4:3–6

Meditation: This is the morning that I ask the question, "What is my excuse?" What a relevant question for this Advent Season. A season of hope, love, and positive possibilities for living life to its fullest. Excuses are easily made when we live apart from the illuminate light of God, who is Jesus Christ. God has removed every excuse that would cause us to stumble. Thank God today for the light of knowledge that leads us to the light of God's glory, the face of Jesus Christ. Let us love again, let us hope again, let us live again, and let us shine again. Let us pray!

Prayer: Our convincing God, who by your mercy and grace has shown yourself true through your profound promises in your Word. Bless me that I may become a vessel boldly standing to proclaim the light of your Word to the unbelievers I encounter each day. Plant me firmly in your Word. In the name of the light of the world, Jesus! Amen!

Daily Reflections

What does the scripture mean to me?

____

____

____

____

____

How will I apply this meditation and bring light to my day?

____
____
____
____
____

What will I be able to share with others to help them to know Christ?

____
____
____
____
____

Tuesday Thought for Today: Greater is he that is in me than any adversarial force in this world.

Scripture: 1 John 1:4–7

Meditation: The declaration of this Epistle is clear and that is "the light is without darkness!" If we belong to God, are in love and charity with our neighbors, and have the desire to lead a new life in Christ, we are people of light. As people of light, we walk in the light of God. This light brings fellowship with God and with his Son, Jesus Christ our Lord. Those who live without the light are those who want their deeds covered by the darkness of ignorance, fear, and unbelief. There is no mistake. Believe that God is life, God is light, and God is love. Let us pray!

Prayer: O great God, precious God, you are greater than anything. Great God, bless me in the midst of the forces of this world to always remember that though Satan runs rampart through the world, *you* in me will be able to overpower the tricks of the enemy. Get thee behind me, Satan! You are a defeated. Thank you God for Holy Ghost power, wonder working power! Hallelujah! Amen!

Daily Reflections

What does the scripture mean to me?

____

____

____

____

____

How will I apply this meditation and bring light to my day?

____

____

____

____

____

What will I be able to share with others to help them to know Christ?

____

____

____

____

____

Wednesday: Thought for Today: The depth of God's love for us is greater than our understanding.

Scripture: John 3:16–21

Meditation: The deeds of evil persons are covered up by the darkness of sin and ignorance of the truth. Evil deeds hate the light, but thanks be to God who has given light to the world. The person who receives the light receives the truth and that truth is the word of God made flesh to shine among us. The word of light, life, and truth is Jesus the Christ. Please take a moment and share this truth in order for someone to accept the light today. Let us pray!

Prayer: Dear God, I am in awe of your love for me! Even though I know you love me I am still awestricken that you chose me. Thank you, God, for sending your Son Jesus to light this dark world, ensuring my place in glory with you. Thank you, Jesus! Amen!

Daily Reflections

What does the scripture mean to me?

____
____
____
____
____

How will I apply this meditation and bring light to my day?

____
____
____
____
____

What will I be able to share with others to help them to know Christ?

____
____
____
____
____

Thursday: Thought for Today: God gives comfort and strength.

Scripture: Isaiah 40:1–11

Meditation: The Isaiah text in this fourteenth chapter begins with a resounding proclamation, "Comfort, comfort, my people says our God!" The prophecy of Israel's deliverance from ungodly rule and suffering would be foretold. The challenges that people of God face today will not be able to stand up against the Word of God. Heaven and earth shall pass away but God's Word will remain forever. Be encouraged today that God's Word will stand up, build up, and straighten you up. God's Word is forever! His name is Jesus! Let us pray!

Tell anyone today that "my hope is built on nothing less than Jesus blood and righteousness!" Thank you, God, thank you, Jesus! Let us pray!

Prayer: God of light and love, you light up my life! Thank you for giving me hope to carry on in the darkest of days. Thank you, Lord, for Jesus, the light of my salvation, the light of my hope, the light of my joy, the joy of my heart. I give you praise! In the precious name of Jesus I pray. Amen

Daily Reflections

What does the scripture mean to me?

____

____

____

____

____

How will I apply this meditation and bring light to my day?

____

____

____

____

____

What will I be able to share with others to help them to know Christ?

____

____

____

____

____

Friday Thought for Today: Jesus is the way.

Scripture: Isaiah 2:1–5

Meditation: Come, my Father's children, let us walk in the light of the Lord. What a great day when we seek always to walk in God's light. This will be the day that nations will not strike down or oppose one another. This will be the day when we will ascend the mountain of the Lord's temple and allow him to teach us his ways and his will that we might live together as humankind. I can now hear the echoes of shouts of joy declaring, "Great day the righteous marching; great day the righteous marching; God's going to build up Zion's wall." Come, my Father's children. Let us walk in the light of the Lord. Let us pray!

Prayer: Dear God, you are the peace in my spirit and the joy in my heart. I love you, dear Lord. I pray that the promise of peace will be witnessed by all the people of the earth. May your guiding Holy Spirit dwell among your people from this time forth and forevermore. In the name of Jesus I pray. Amen

Daily Reflections

What does the scripture mean to me?

____

____

____

____

____

How will I apply this meditation and bring light to my day?

____

____

____

____

____

What will I be able to share with others to help them to know Christ?

____

____

____

____

____

Saturday Thought for Today: All these blessings are mine!

Scripture: Luke 2:25–33

Meditation: Praise God from whom all blessings flow, praise him all creatures here below. Praise him above ye heavenly host, praise Father, Son, and Hoy Ghost—Amen. If you have seen the Lord's Christ, praise God. If you have seen the glory of the Lord, praise God. This day is the Christ-Mass when we celebrate the birth of Jesus who is our Emmanuel. When our hopes and dreams are realized, we ought to shout to the glory of God. When God's promises are fulfilled in our lives tell the good news everywhere. The praise of Simeon harmonizes with my praise, "For my eyes have seen your salvation…a light for revelation to the Gentiles and for glory to your people Israel." Let us pray!

Prayer: I will bless you, O Lord, with all my soul and all that is within me! I will bless your holy name! You are worthy, O Lord, and I give you all the praise! Gracious Lord, I give you praise! Thank you for blessing me with the glorious gift of your darling Son, Jesus Christ! *Glory to your name*! *Amen*! *Amen*! *Amen*!

Daily Reflections

What does the scripture mean to me?

____

____

____

____

____

How will I apply this meditation and bring light to my day?

____

____

____

____

____

What will I be able to share with others to help them to know Christ?

____

____

____

____

____

Week IV

Light the Candle of: Peace

Sunday: Thought for Today: God unifies us through his Word.

Scripture: Romans 15:4–13

Meditation: Today begins the last week of the Advent (a-coming) of our Christian witness. "What trouble have we seen, what conflicts have we passed; fighting and fears within and without." These words are a few lines from one of the great hymns of the church. During this season of our Christian witness we are reminded that God unifies his church through his Word and abiding presence. He gives us the Word to encourage us and remind us that we are one in Christ who gives us the spirit of unity. No matter what the struggle within or without, we persevere and build up one another. Be encouraged and excited because of the God of Hope who is our Christ, our Lord and our Savior. Let us pray!

Prayer: O God of comfort and patience, grant that we may ever lean on your comforting Word to bring unity among us. In the precious name of Jesus I pray. Amen

Daily Reflections

What does the scripture mean to me?

____
____
____
____
____

How will I apply this meditation and bring light to my day?

____
____
____
____
____

What will I be able to share with others to help them to know Christ?

____
____
____
____
____

Monday: Thought for Today: God delivers us from the ungodly.

Scripture: Psalms 43:3–6

Meditation: Shout, for deliverance is yours! Shout, for the joy of Christ is your strength and hope! Be comforted in this day that God sends forth his light and truth to lead us to his will and his way. We have not one adversary, which the power and presence of the Holy Spirit will not destroy. Whatever the temptation, trial, or test, go to God, our joy and our delight. Shout for deliverance is yours! Praise God for deliverance is yours! Praise God this morning! Let us pray!

Prayer: God of deliverance, in the world where the enemy runs rampart, let us run from the traps of the wicked into your sacred places of protection. Accept us as we seek your face. In the precious name of Jesus I pray. Amen

Daily Reflections

What does the scripture mean to me?

____

____

____

____

____

How will I apply this meditation and bring light to my day?

____

____

____

____

____

What will I be able to share with others to help them to know Christ?

Tuesday: Thought for Today: The Lord is my light and my salvation.

Scripture: Psalms 27:1–4

Meditation: This new morning with its new mercies, join in with saints around the world in this exciting declaration of faith. "The Lord is my light and my salvation, whom shall I fear? The Lord is the stronghold of my life, of whom shall I be afraid?" This new day, step out boldly in faith. Hold your head up, square your shoulders, and seek the Lord. Today, speak a word of faith on behalf of the men and women whose lives are on the line in Afghanistan. Today, let us stand in the gap for those families who grieve over the senseless deaths of loved ones in every city in America. Let us pray for the just men and women that have been sworn to protect our country. Today, speak a word of hope for the families of those men and women on distant shores fighting for freedom. Today, stand in the gap for the families of incarcerated men and women who need to know that the Lord is our light and our salvation. Let us pray!

Prayer: O God of protection and power, thank you for saving me. Because I trust in you, Lord, I fear no evil because I know you are with me. Forever keep me in the path of your light. Amen

Daily Reflections

What does the scripture mean to me?

____

____

____

____

____

How will I apply this meditation and bring light to my day?

___

___

___

___

___

What will I be able to share with others to help them to know Christ?

___

___

___

___

___

Wednesday: Thought for Today: The Word of God guides our feet and gives light for life's journey.

Scripture: Psalm 119:105–106

Meditation: During this season of Advent we are guided on life's journey by the light of God which is Jesus, "the Anointed Christ of God." Let us share the Word of God with others that their pathways will be lighted. The Word of God is in us and we are in the Word of God. Share the word and share self with others to the glory of God. Let us pray!

Prayer: O magnificent Father, living Word, lead me in a plain path. Lead me to the light of your Word. In the precious name of Jesus I pray. Amen

Daily Reflections

What does the scripture mean to me?

____

____

____

____

____

How will I apply this meditation and bring light to my day?

____

____

____

____

____

What will I be able to share with others to help them to know Christ?

____

____

____

____

____

Thursday: Thought for Today: Walk in the light.

Scripture: John 12:35–36

Meditation: Praise the Lord! Praise the Lord! The people who walk in the light know where they are going. This Johannine text briefly yet powerfully directs the people of God to place our trust in the light, that we will become people of light. The light of God is transforming and transparent. The light of God changes us; however, the light itself remains the same. This light is past, present, and future. The light is the "Anointed Christ of God…he is from everlasting to everlasting." Hallelujah, Amen. Let us pray!

Prayer: Savior, let me walk with thee in lowly paths of service free. Tell me the secret to help me bear the strain of toil, the fret of care. In hope that sends a shining ray, far down the future's broadening way. In peace that brings a transformed mind. O savior let me walk with Thee. In the name of Jesus I pray. Amen

Daily Reflections

What does the scripture mean to me?

____

____

____

____

____

How will I apply this meditation and bring light to my day?

____

____

____

____

____

What will I be able to share with others to help them to know Christ?

____

____

____

____

____

Friday: Thought for Today: Let us reprove our brothers and sisters and lead them to the light.

Scripture: Ephesians 5:6–14

Meditation: This morning, O sleeper, awake and arise from the dungeon of sin, guilt, and shame. Arise and be penitent for your day of recovery and cleaning is near. The Light of God shines upon you that you may now walk and live in the light. The Apostle Paul declares that "the fruit of the light consist in all goodness, righteousness, and truth." This fruit pleases the Lord. The darkness of night is past. The light of our Lord's Christ is upon us. Let us pray!

Prayer: God of grace and God of glory, let us so live our lives to be a living example for those who are walking in darkness. Let us be a living example, a light to lead them out of the darkness of sin to the light of your spirit. In the matchless name of Jesus I pray. Amen

Daily Reflections

What does the scripture mean to me?

____

____

____

____

____

How will I apply this meditation and bring light to my day?

____

____

____

____

____

What will I be able to share with others to help them to know Christ?

____

____

____

____

____

Saturday: Thought for Today: We are God's chosen people.

Scripture: 1 Peter 2:5–9

Meditation: Rejoice, rejoice! Aren't you glad this good morning? Aren't you mighty glad this morning? Know ye this day that God has called you out of darkness into his wonderful light. This light, chosen by God, and offered by God, and precious to God has become the chief corner stone. Will you trust him today? Will you be built up in him today? God has promised that you will never be put to shame. Rejoice; praise him today, you who are God's chosen people. Let us pray!

Prayer: Omniscient God, my heavenly Father, you could have chosen anyone else in the world to be adopted into your family. Thank you for choosing me! Thank you for your favor toward me! Hallelujah! Hallelujah! Amen!

Daily Reflections

What does the scripture mean to me?

____

____

____

____

____

How will I apply this meditation and bring light to my day?

____

____

____

____

____

What will I be able to share with others to help them to know Christ?

About the Authors

Rev. Dr. Mary A. Hudson is a thriving entrepreneur and the president and CEO of a speech pathology private practice. She works closely with Isaac in the ministry of the church.

Rev. Dr. Isaac N. Hudson, II has served as pastor of congregations in Arkansas, Georgia, Oklahoma, and Alabama. He currently serves as senior pastor of Nichols Chapel AME Church in Phenix City, Alabama. He is a dedicated pastor, preacher, and teacher.

Their partnership in marriage and ministry has spanned over forty years. The Hudsons have four children, five grandchildren, and one great grandchild. They both enjoy spending time together, preaching, teaching, writing, and working in the yard.

CPSIA information can be obtained
at www.ICGtesting.com
Printed in the USA
LVHW032257181220
674517LV00005B/689

About the Author

RON KUBAN HAS EXTENSIVE EXPERIENCE with Edmonton's community league movement. For over twenty years, he has served in many capacities including his local community league, the area council, and the Edmonton Federation of Community Leagues (EFCL). At the league level, Ron served in various Board positions and was involved in diverse projects from community beautification to playground and park development. As a member, and later chair of the Mill Woods Presidents' Council, he also co-chaired three of the council's Canada Day celebrations, which in 2004 attracted more than 45,000 visitors. From 1999 to 2002, he served as president of the EFCL during its revitalization.

Ron Kuban has volunteered for many community-based organizations including the Mill Woods Community Patrol (founding member), the Mill Woods Soccer Association (board member, coach), and the Edmonton Regional Crime Prevention Network Society (founding chair).

Ron Kuban graduated with a BA from the Royal Military College of Canada as well as an MEd and a PhD from the University of Alberta. In 2003, he received the Queen's Jubilee medal for his community service.